BEing

The Titus Concept

Al Diaz

1st WORLD PUBLISHING

BEing

The Titus Concept

Al Diaz

© Al Diaz 2008

Published by 1stWorld Publishing
P.O. Box 2211 Fairfield, Iowa 52556
tel: 641-209-5000 • fax: 641-209-3001
web: www.1stworldpublishing.com

First Edition

LCCN: 2008941036
SoftCover ISBN: 978-1-4218-9042-5
HardCover ISBN: 978-1-4218-9041-8
eBook ISBN: 978-1-4218-9043-2

This material has been written and published solely for educational purposes. The author and the publisher shall have neither liability nor responsibility to any person or entity with respect to any loss, damage or injury caused or alleged to be caused directly or indirectly by the information contained in this book.

"Al Diaz has a way of expressing profound Truths in powerfully simple ways. What many authors take volumes to say, Al can communicate more clearly in just a few pages. What's even better is that Al's passion for helping others can literally be felt as you read his material. BEing the Titus Concept continues this pattern and brings together many spiritual Truths in a way that makes them easy to understand and put into practice. I love the way Al describes how to truly love yourself, and how this will improve every aspect of your life."
—Alan Tutt, author of Choose To Believe: A Practical Guide to Living Your Dreams. www.PowerKeysPub.com

"From the moment you pick this book up you feel a vibrant energy that courses through your entire body energizing every atom and molecule to magnetically attract abundance. Mr. Diaz has created a tour de force that should be read by everyone who is in pursuit of personal and professional success"
—Nick Arrizza M.D. http://telecoaching4u.com

"Al Diaz has created the Ultimate "TOOL FOR YOUR SOUL" with the Titus Concept. These simple steps will enhance your BEing and help you create positive change with rewarding results. If every soul had this from day one of life, our world would be a better place. The Titus Concept is a gift to ourselves from ourselves through you! Thank you Al, you are our gift!"
—Marisa Ryan, Speaker and Intuitive Life Coach
www.marisaryan.com

In dedication and in memory of *Socorro Diaz*
December 05, 1928—April 16th, 2008

This book is dedicated to my mom Socorro Diaz who throughout her Life persevered and managed to have the best to her ability. Through all of her experiences for the most part she would come out on top of the world and she would beat the odds.

Thank you mom for all of your Love, support, assistance, and guidance throughout my Life, including with all of my future experiences that have yet to come.

I kNow you are one of my biggest cheerleaders and I am forever grateful.

As you always said
"For our best and highest good"

I agree

Love you…across all boundaries.

Acknowledgements

My wife Gloria, thank you for all of your Love and guidance through all of our experiences. We will continue to grow and emanate our Light for the best and highest good of all.

My daughter Vanessa, thank you for BEing my hero and what our future generations are already BEcoming.

All of my mentors, guides, and teachers that have supported, assisted and guided me to BE who I am today, especially White Eagle and Dawna Su, thank you.

My support group of "Conscious Directors" that are taking The Titus Concept and creating a critical mass to BE awakened, an ascension wave of a mass collective process where there is mass insight, revelation, change and the choice of moving into another realm or way of living life, each time becoming more simplistic, with an awareness of a new reality and its heart-centered values. Thank you Gloria Diaz, Karen Payton, Pomaika`i Coulon, Raul Rosiles, and Henry Guerra.

Thank you Annie Anderson and Maria Lajvort for the design and editing of the original "BEing The Titus Concept" you are a big reason of where the book is today.

Lynn Caceres thank you for capturing my essence with your photos.

Ed Spinella and Rodney Charles thank you for this opportunity and blessing.

1st World Publishing simply rocks!

From my Heart and from the Creator
Right Now and in every moment
Every cell of my body
Every level of my consciousness
Every area of my BEing
And every part of my mind
With expressed appreciation and joy
I already am living the blessings of the energy, essence and
quality of Life
That caused me to even more Love and adore
My inner spirit and my inner resources
For only welcoming the wisdom and gifts of the soulmates,
guides, and beings
Who are 100% God's Love and Light
And whose only purpose is to assist me to awaken
To the extraordinary magnificence of my true nature and destiny
And having the required and desired experiences and essential
resources
That are compatible to my Heart's desires and God's Love
Supplement my power
To have healed, blessed, and empowered as
many as people as possible
Including my Self
For our best and highest good
Thank you Spirit.

—Comfirmation by **Al Diaz**

Table of Contents

In Brief

You have allowed this book into your Life. You are already BEing what this book is all about. But consider those two sentences you just read a little more closely, and think of this: you are allowing or BEing this book either deliberately or unconsciously.

If you are allowing or BEing this book unconsciously, then you are living Life on a whim, probably through ego. But if you are deliberately allowing and BEing this book in your Life, then pass it onto someone else who can use it, because you have the Awareness to live your Life for your best and highest good.

The value of this book is what it is DOing to enhance Life for the best and highest good of all.

My intention is to have one million plus people world-wide living and functioning even more effortlessly and as simply as possible, in other words, 'BEing The Titus Concept'.

This book is circulating around the world with the Power and Energy of the Universe supporting it.

It is short.

It is direct.

It is powerful.

This book is divided into three sections, the first section preps you for The Titus Concept which are chapters 1 through 3, the second section deals with the aspects of The Titus Concept which are chapters 4 through 9, and the last section containing chapters 10 and 11 has a powerful resource and my final thoughts.

There are also confirmations that I have written and placed strategically within this book. They are very personal, powerful, and are meant to guide.

Deep down you already kNow everything written in this book. It is simply guiding you to remember what you already kNow or accelerating your Awareness, and as you do there are journaling pages at the end of each chapter for the "ahas", thoughts, or comments you may have.

For OUR best and highest good, all ways... It is time and we deserve it.

Ilumine Ao,

Al Diaz

Introduction

I am writing this book to share my experiences with you so that you may benefit. I am now fifty one years old, but for the first forty plus years of my Life it was one heck of a roller coaster ride. Somewhere along the line, I started to get it right or better said—I started to raise my level of awareness.

After awhile, I realized that raising my level of awareness also introduced me to spirituality (I don't mean religion) and I was also moving forward in that area. With the exception of my wife and other like minded people, I wouldn't mention the term 'spiritual' around just anybody. Not because I was embarrassed, but because I was still trying to comprehend what awareness and spirituality were all about.

One day, a close family member and I were e-mailing back and forth, and out of nowhere he brought up the word spiritual. I was shocked that he even knew the word, so we went back and forth and talked about where our level of awareness was at that time. Finally I asked him "Why didn't you ever tell me any of this before?" His reply was, "You weren't ready."

Though I didn't tell him then, and he will find out when he reads this, I was shocked that he told me that! So much so, that I was even a little perturbed that he would have considered I was not ready, especially since I really needed this information during those first forty years.

Eventually, I realized that he was right. I wasn't ready, because I was living through my ego, though I wasn't aware that was what I was doing at the time. I just thought what I was going through all those years was how Life is supposed to be, some have what it takes, some don't, some are lucky, some are unlucky.

Until…

I started to read books like this one.

I started to listen to others who seemed to know a little bit more than I did.

Almost every time I understood something, I had a burning desire to learn more and go to the next level. I even realized at some point that there is better way to raise your level of awareness rather than learning to do so. I will explain that in a later chapter.

The experiences I have had since September of 2002 and continuing through to this very moment are astronomical. Anytime prior to that date I could not have dreamed or conceived everything that has transpired for me since then. It was all brought on by consciously and deliberately raising my awareness.

What if some one told you that by raising your level of awareness you could have what you desire and require in Life? By accelerating your awareness and with some guidance, you could have powerful meditations, great relationships, find skilled mentors, a home that you desire, or you could fulfill a long or short term vision that you've had. These are the types of scenarios that can happen for just about anybody who is willing to become more aware and be guided.

As you continue to raise your vibration through your awareness it creates a snowball effect, with more people coming into your Life that at one time you wouldn't dare dream of meeting, more resources, more support, and even more guidance. Just when you think you have peaked, along will come some more inspiration because you are so wide open to accepting, that your Life will accelerate even more.

All of this can happen, I kNow, because it did for me. It happened for me by raising my level of awareness and can also happen for you. Please understand we are equals, we are all perfect as who and what we are, the only difference is our level of awareness.

In December of 2006 I received more inspiration (that is what this book is about) and I began having an almost immediate response to the process, from having magnificent opportunities presenting themselves to Now having a very aware and gifted mentors guiding me to the next level of my Life journey.

The one thing that I can vouch for is that the type of people who come into your Life through your heightened awareness will be amazing. You could meet the Dahli Lama, or meet and talk with Dr. Wayne Dyer. Even nature can reflect your heightened vibration by swimming with dolphins.

You could become certified in Usui Reiki II by a very gifted and spiritual individual from the Andes of Peru, even though you never dreamed or thought of doing it, all because of your heightened awareness! Out of nowhere he could appear in your Life, to guide your current part of your journey.

People will appear seemingly out of nowhere and every-where, and then basically tell you that they are here to support you on your path and in your endeavors.

All of these events have actually happened in my Life. I am not telling you of my experiences to brag about it, or for you to consider that I am lucky. I am telling you of these events to let you kNow that amazing things like this can absolutely happen in your Life as well!

If you were standing before me I would look into your eyes and tell you that all these and even greater events can happen to and for you. That is, if you are ready…

"The day I received Al's new book, I sat down and read it all the way through in one sitting. I couldn't put it down! I love how Al gives solid packed concise straight—on wisdom—gold on each page. And I am going to read BEing The Titus Concept again."
—Gloria Wendroff, Heavenletters™ Love Letters from God, Book One. www.heavenletters.org

"Once again, in his down to earth, easily understand-able way, Al Diaz gives us some amazing keys to having and being what we desire. This book takes the Titus Concept right into every moment of our daily lives. In today's world, we are all so busy and over-whelmed and what is wonderful about what Al gives us, is that it is do-able in the course of all of the other things we have to do each day. These tools, in my opinion, are unpretentious but powerful 'Companions for Transformation' on one's journey through life. Thank you my dear friend and mentor."
—Paula Shaw, Author of Chakras, The Magnificent Seven and From Tears to Triumph, Creator of Conscious Healing and Repatterning Therapy (CHART). www.paulashaw.net

Journal

Are you ready? Explain why…

_____

_____

_____

_____

_____

_____

_____

_____

_____

_____

_____

_____

_____

_____

_____

_____

From my Heart and from the Creator
Right Now and in every moment
Every cell of my body
Every level of my consciousness
Every area of my Being
And every part of my mind
With expressed appreciation and Joy
I am living the blessings of the energy, essence
and quality of Life
As a Loving co-creator to my Self
Freely utilizing God's gift of Love, healing and empowerment
To create, change and/or shift any area or level of my Life
As I desire or require
BEing the joy of giving to others and my Self
And the joy of receiving from others and my Self
God's blessings in abundance
Experiencing all of what I already have from within my Heart
For my best and highest good
And for the best and highest good of all
Thank you Spirit.

—Comfirmation by **Al Diaz**

Answers

I am going to be upfront and direct with you right now. I may even offend some of your beliefs that your ego holds onto dearly.

Ready?

If anyone or anything ever tells you "I have the answers, come and follow me." RUN—in the opposite direction! If you do follow someone or something that you think has the answers you are seeking, your Life will be a roller coaster ride. Think about it - how many times have you done something because you thought someone else had the answers? How successful were you? How long did it last? Did it work to your satisfaction?

The best anyone or anything can do for you is to guide you. That's it! That includes me.

You know why?

YOU already have the answers!!!

The answers are already within you!!!

So how can anyone or anything tell you they have the

answers when you already do? Does that make sense?

There are two ways I can show you that you have every conceivable answer you require within you.

The first one is more concrete, logical, and scientific.

Do you know what DNA is? It is intelligence that is in every cell of your body.

Where does DNA come from? It comes from your parents, who acquired it from their parents.

In other words, your DNA or intelligence that is in every cell of your body comes from all of your ancestors, from the beginning of your lineage. That is what makes you special. That is what makes you unique. That is why you are you.

So what does that mean to you?

Every conceivable experience, thought, action, feeling, emotion, decision, choice, belief, intention, attitude, knowledge, piece of information or wisdom that your ancestors had is stored in your DNA. So there really is no possible experience you could have that someone at sometime in your ancestry has not already had, in one form or another, at some point in time, and probably many times, by many of them.

You have access to all of that intelligence.

Here is the second reason why you already have all the answers.

This is more on the metaphysical / spiritual angle.

We all have a connection to a higher power. You can call it The Universe, Source, God, Spirit, Buddha, Allah, Jesus, Mohammed, Nature, All That Is or whatever you desire to call it/him/her.

The phrase that I like to use is "The Creator of all creation".

That higher power, that creative force, has all the answers —and we are all connected to that intelligence.

How?

Everything in this Universe is energy, absolutely everything. That means you are energy, that higher power is energy, and it is not a separate energy. The only difference is the frequency or vibration of the energy.

Your vibration that comes from within you (your Heart) is what connects to the Higher Power, the Higher Power that has all the intelligence, all the answers, and is the Creator of all creation.

Here is a simple metaphor for this. If you plug a radio into a wall socket and tap into the electricity the radio will turn on and you can then switch to any channel that you desire to hear, and listen. If you unplug the radio and go to another room, plug it in to another wall socket, tap into the electricity and again the radio will turn on and you can switch to any channel you desire to hear.

Just like plugging into any wall socket for electricity for your radio, you can also use your own energy to connect with or tap into the energy of the Creator of all creation at any time and any place. What matters here is that the energy or vibration you emanate is what you will get in return from Spirit. The absolute best way to do this is to consciously and deliberately have your energy and vibration as high as possible in every moment. That is how you tap into the higher vibration of Spirit. I trust that by the time you are done reading this book you will have the ability to do so even more simply and effortlessly, with the One with all the answers.

What if we used these two paths of inner Wisdom and put them together?

Can you imagine how powerful that would BE?!!

Since we are tapping into our own inner Wisdom for the answers, which means the answers already exist, then we are not learning. Rather, we are just simply remembering the "Truth" that is already within us, and the "Truth" of who and what we truly are: The spark of Spirit and the master of our own Life. Remembering these "Truths" will lead you to co-create your journey in Life in every moment, together as one with Spirit, as master, and with your own inner Wisdom.

"BEing The Titus Concept is a must read. It will inspire and awaken you to new levels of existence never thought possible. Al Diaz speaks from his soul and is truly a spiritual warrior for the light. Trust that his words will transform your life."
—Bonny Cheryl, Ordained Spiritual Reverend, Anchoress for the Light. mystikamoon@yahoo.com

"Being The Titus Concept is a delightful journal/workbook for classically conditioning oneself through self-oriented insightful processes, affirmations, and steps. Through these, one is led to move into self-empowerment in a simple and basic way that even the beginners on their journey to self-evolution can easily follow. As one moves on in these procedures one is prompted to overcome negative impressions and perceptions from one's past, live and honor one's present and thus create a magnetically induced powerful future by becoming that future internally first. One is urged to view all experiences with gratitude and thanks. When one appreciates that they co-create from within and look at all experiences and individuals with gratitude for what has been taught, one is impressed to reach for one's best and highest good at all moments. Through sharing his own personal analogies and story of his growth into awareness, Al Diaz has made this a personal good journey. Bless and thank you,"
—Rev. Jean Holmes, www.higherwisdom.com

Journal

Three Processes to Raise your Vibration and Energy For Your Self

Now you kNow that everything and anything is energy.

Would you like to kNow how to find out what your current vibration and energy levels are?

Would you like to kNow what you are emanating to the Universe?

For the next few days look around you.

Who are your friends?

What are your resources?

Who are your contacts?

Who are your guides, teachers, and mentors?

Who are your acquaintances?

How are your relationships?

The answers to those questions will tell you what your current energy vibration is. It will tell you exactly what it is that the Universe and those around you are receiving. Let's add the Law of Attraction into this. Since your vibration is what you will attract to your Self, doesn't it make sense for you to raise your vibration and energy to the highest possible level?

How about having a Life journey that continues to get better and better?

I am going to tell you something that is required for you to have the ability to raise your vibration. How you feel about your Self is an exact match to what you will get out of Life. How you see your Self is how others will see you. What you do for your Self is what others will do for you. Most importantly what is going on inside of you is what the Universe will give you.

It is that simple!

Here is my personal version of the Law of Attraction: Spirit loves you so much that it will give you exactly what is going on inside of you. In other words, how you feel, what you see, and what you do for your Self is exactly what Spirit will give you.

So what is the #1 thing you must DO or BE?

Love and Honor

Love your Self unconditionally and honor who you are and what you are. Both are critical to how your journey in Life will BE.

Honestly, how much do you Love your Self?

Do you even know?

Have you even thought about it?

Is it 10%? Maybe 70%? Is your Life almost perfect and you're sitting at 90%?

I was over 40 years old when I figured out how much I loved my Self, and it was closer to 10% rather than 90%. Before then, nobody really took the time to show me, and I just didn't put in the effort to figure it out. I guess you can say I was asleep thinking that this how Life is supposed to be.

Whatever you feel about your Self will have an effect on all of the following:

- Your level of self esteem.
- The freedom you have in all areas and levels of your Life.
- The ability and the degree to forgive and love others and your Self.

We all come into this Life with core values (not learned values like ambition, greed, jealousy, hatred). These core values are what reside within our own Heart. But, how you feel about your Self and how much you Love your Self will also determine the level at which these values will reside or emanate in your Life. Here are some core values:

Peace

Happiness

Joy

Intimacy

Understanding

Prosperity

Success

Wealth

Health

Harmony

Faith

Honesty

Right Action

Courage

Confidence

Patience

Commitment

Focus

Awareness

Intuition

Abundance

Trust

Inner Knowing

Freedom

Creativity

Spiritual Growth

Inner Power

Gratitude

I'm sure you can think of other core values that are important to you. (Please write them down for a later chapter)

Are any of the above core values especially important to you?

Do you desire to have them at even higher levels in your Life?

The following simple way of raising your vibration and energy has been taught in varying degrees in workshops, seminars and teleseminars that I have attended. The feedback I have received along with what it has done for me in my Life is incredible! You will be amazed at how your Life will automatically shift.

Here it is:

Love your Self unconditionally.

That doesn't mean you do it from an ego standpoint, but from your Heart.

Honor who you are and what you are.

In Spirit's eyes you are absolutely perfect. This is how you must see and feel about your Self.

So how do you go about doing this?

It's very simple, but for some it will require a lot of courage. For others it will take telling their ego to back off, because ego will try and convince them how stupid this is and that it doesn't work.

For the next 30 days do the following:

Right before you go to bed go to a mirror and look deep "into" your eyes (not "at" your eyes), take three deep breaths, and tell your Self I love you unconditionally 3 times, then tell your Self I honor who you are and what you are 3 times, then go to sleep.

As soon as you wake up go to a mirror and look deep into your eyes (not at your eyes), take three deep breaths, and tell your Self I love you unconditionally (3 times) then tell your Self I honor who you are and what you are (3 times), then get ready for your day.

The more uncomfortable or silly this feels when you first do it, will indicate how little you Love your Self. At the other end of the spectrum, the more comfortable and good you feel when doing it, will indicate how much you DO Love your Self.

It does not matter where you are right Now. What does matter is where you will be 30 days from Now.

By practicing this simple technique for thirty days, your Life will have begun to shift, and your vibration and energy will have been raised to your benefit.

Start tonight.

It is time and you deserve it.

Gratitude

Be grateful for every conceivable thing in your Life. It does not matter what it is. What does matter is that you are grateful for absolutely everything. To get you over the hump of things happening in your Life that you would prefer to not have happening, understand this: in every single moment of your Life there is either a blessing or an opportunity. There is no third option. You either co-created the blessing or it's an opportunity of some sort, most likely to grow in some way.

Yes, I know… sometimes you won't understand how a certain situation can be either a blessing or an opportunity. This has happened to me many times. In those moments and sometimes somewhat frustrated, I just tell my Self "Where is the blessing and opportunity in all of this? I just don't get it. Right now, I don't understand…" and you know what? Somehow that gets me back to trusting, which leads to being grateful, with the inner kNowing that my understanding is yet to come.

How many times in your Life has something happened

that you really didn't care for, but after a length of time has passed you understood why the situation transpired the way it did? When you have this realization, you end up being incredibly grateful for that moment in your journey of Life.

When you emanate gratitude, gratitude is what will be given right back to you. Since that is what you are emanating, that is what the Universe will respond to. The more appreciative and thankful you are the more blessings will be given to you. That is how Spirit works!

Have you ever given something to someone and they show no appreciation or even say thank you? Does that enhance the feeling of giving them something again when the opportunity arises?

Think about this: Could it be that Spirit senses your vibrational energy of gratitude and responds accordingly?

If that is the case, then it makes sense to be in loving gratitude and forever grateful for all things and all areas of your Life.

Life is a mirror

At every level of your Life and in every area of your Life, what you see, touch, smell, taste, hear, and sense is all coming from within you.

Does that make sense? If not, it's alright; most people don't get it or don't believe it. I know I didn't at first. It took me a while to put my ego aside, and stop blaming and faulting others and myself.

Here's a tip: get rid of the words fault and blame from your vocabulary. If you continue to use them, they will continue to disempower you. So take your power back and stop using them.

Here is a simple way to look at your Life being a mirror of what is going on inside of you.

Imagine you or your body as a movie projector, the camera lenses is coming out of your chest, the film is circulating within your body, and the screen that the movie is playing on is your Life story that is played out in front of you everyday.

Do you know what is in that film?

The accumulation of all the experiences you have had since you were born.

What do all of those experiences add up to?

Your ego.

What is your ego?

It is all of the attitudes, beliefs, emotions, feelings, thoughts, actions, patterns and everything else you have consciously or unconsciously accepted from others and yourself, including DNA, organizations and institutions.

Depending on who you listen to, it is estimated that 3-7% of the world's population is fully aware. That means about 93% of the population accepts what is going on in their lives as 'Truth'! Some of that 'Truth' is based on the junk that the ego has accepted through all of their Life experiences, whether they were valid for them or not!

The film is corrupted! Do you see?!!!

Yet, that is the film that is running inside of you and projecting out to your external reality. The film is an accumulation of all the experiences you've had, with the ego using them to go into survival mode to keep you moving forward, and supposedly even protecting you.

You know what that is called? FEAR

Think about it.

I am willing to guess that many of your choices and decisions are fear based.

You don't do this or don't do that because you remember the pain, scar and hurt of a prior experience. Through the ego you don't allow the good that Life has to offer into your Life, because the ego is supposedly protecting you.

Your 10th grade teacher may have told you that you will be a success! Yet ten years later you are looking for a job that fulfills you, while being at a job you are unhappy at. All the while your ego is reminding you how successful you are because at least you have a job.

This is just one example of what the ego does for you.

What is the alternative?

Live and function from your Heart.

When you do, your external reality will have a magnificent shift.

These three processes will affect all aspects of your Life, including your level of awareness. But most importantly, how you see and feel about your Self is what you will vibrate and what the Universe will respond to. I attribute all three of these processes to bringing me to this point in my Life, and surrounding me with the Love, support, energy, guidance, and resources that are required and desired for my best and highest good, and the best and highest good of all...

If there is only one thing you get out of this entire book, it should be this:

Love your Self unconditionally, and honor who you are and what you are.

At least for this moment, your vibration and your energy level have brought you to read this book. As I continue to raise my vibration and energy level, it continues to have Spirit bring me higher levels of mentors and All That Is for my best and highest good. You too can surround your Self with mentors and All That Is for your best and highest good, because Spirit reinforces the energy and Love you have for your Self by matching your vibration.

*"Al Diaz writes from his heart many beautiful, simple, yet profound revelations that will heighten your awareness and inspire you to be all you can be in this lifetime. His personal aha moments of spiritual a wakening connect me deeply with my own soul and spiritual connection I feel with Al. This book reminds me that raising my vibration expands my ability to feel Oneness with others who vibrate at a high level to co-create heaven on earth. His passion for life, love, joy, peace and other core qualities leaves me (the reader) with appreciation and gratitude for my (their) own magnificent BEing, guided by spirit and my (their) own divine wisdom. I finished the book having great faith that we are co-creating a world where everyone has the opportunity to be happy, healthy, and successful. Al reminds us that since everything that happens to us is for our best and highest good, there are no mistakes. This helps me accept everything from a higher, more spiritual perspective. Understanding my soul lessons touches my heart and opens to deeper love relationships and the strength to release negative beliefs from the past. **BEing The Titus Concept** is a must read for how to choose your own lifestyle based on who you are as a spiritual BEing on earth to fulfill a divine mission. I thoroughly enjoyed reading it and passing it on to others who will highly benefit from it's positive journey of self-discovery."*
—**Rayna Lumbard, LMFT, InnerSuccess Transformations, Mind/Body/Spirit Therapy, Coaching, and Healing, www.InnerSuccess.com**

Journal

The Chalice

How often have you heard "Is your glass half full or half empty?"

Supposedly your answer to that question will tell you if you are an optimist or a pessimist. Some even say that it indicates if you are a positive or negative thinker.

When we accept those kinds of notions that it is either this or that, or it represents this or that, we have begun the process of limiting ourselves.

Let's try something more useful.

You are in your mothers womb surrounded for the most part with everything you desire and require to nourish you, to grow, and to enhance your Life for the nine or so months you are there. Everything you require is provided for you. You don't have to go searching for anything because everything that is vital for your well being is already there at any time, and as often as you require.

Nine months later it is time to come forth into the external reality that is on the other side of the veil. Right before you do, you get handed a beautiful, glistening, shiny Chalice that has your name on it. You put your little hands around it and you are told to fill it to the brim with 'All That Is' around you, and bring it with you into your new reality. You don't have to worry about spilling any of it, because it is abundant. Your Chalice will always be infinitely filled and over flowing. As you venture forth with your Chalice, you morph with your Chalice and become One with it in your new reality.

I realize there is a lot of symbolism in the above scenario, so let me explain.

The Chalice with your name on it is an indication of who you are and of how special you are - and that your Life is much more than a cup or glass. The 'All That Is' that you filled your Chalice with is the Life force, energy, and essence that you required and desired to sustain you for those nine months, and you have brought that same sustaining Life force into this reality. This Life force is still over flowing from your Chalice.

How do I know?

Would you take your child or a loved one and put them in the middle of a desert with a glass of water that is half full or half empty? Anybody who loves their child absolutely would not! You would probably give them the biggest water tank you could find and give it to them filled to the top with water.

As much as you love your loved ones, it doesn't come close to matching how much the Creator of all creation Loves it's creation. It created you! You were created out of Love! That is why your Chalice has never been less than over-flowing, and will never be less than overflowing. It will always have that Life force to sustain you and keep you moving forward and growing.

Progressing, expanding, moving forward and growing is the natural state for all of creation. It is the natural state for all of creation to become the fullest and grandest expression of itself. Think about this for a moment and realize that everything grows. It doesn't matter if it's a star, an animal, a plant, or even bacteria. Everything is in a natural state of growth or expansion.

Through the Love of Spirit, the Universe provides all things - the energy of Life, the essence of Life, the spirit of Life and the Life force to sustain the growth, so that all can become its fullest and grandest expression, and that includes us humans! But you know what makes us unique from everything else? We get to choose and decide if we desire to grow and move forward. We have free will and free choice. We get to decide if we desire to drink from our abundant Chalice, or if our Chalice is becoming empty.

But, if we choose to kNow and trust that Spirit will always provide and have our Chalice overflowing, then we are allowing Spirit to move us forward and doing so with Love. After all, it is our natural state to grow and succeed, just as when we were in our mother's womb. We had it all then, and we have it all Now. We just need to raise our awareness to see it.

So enough of this half full, half empty nonsense.

Drink from your own unique and special Chalice, that has everything you desire and require in abundance for you to grow, move forward, and expand for your best and highest good.

Imagine, visualize and tell your Self this:

As I drink from my own gifted, unique and special

Chalice, I hydrate every cell in my body, every level of my consciousness, every area of my BEing, and every part of my mind with 'All That Is' for my best and highest good. Thank you Spirit.

Confirmation by Al Diaz

"Al Diaz has written a book of wonders.
We can all take up the challenge The Titus Concept offers and BEcome our full potential for the best and highest good of all
After reading this book, I feel it makes a wonderful gift idea, what better to bless those around you.
Keep in mind the heart and soul these words come from, for the light behind these beautiful words and ideas is the real blessing of Al's work.
Even though I feel this book can become a best seller, I pray that it becomes a "best applied book", put these words into practice!
Now is the time for this book, it will BE a part of the new world that is being born!"
—**Raul Rosiles, founder of Soul Based Living.**
www.soulbasedliving.blogspot.com

"When I sat down to read, "Being the Titus Concept," I was delighted by the easy-to-understand writing style that left me wanting more. There are few books that actually provide new information that can literally change your life. Al Diaz's new book does. I enjoyed having a jour-naling page at the end of each chapter to summarize what was meaningful to me. I had valuable perceptions answering the many insightful questions throughout the book. Al shows how by raising awareness anyone can add to the quality of their life. For example, he describes how to easily raise your vibration and energy. The book is filled with spiritual insight. Al's information provides a very important and progressive step in self discovery. Read the book and find out how you can BE who you were really meant to BE!"
—**Dan Rendsland, Spiritual Mentor and creator of the ONE technique, www.livingfreelovinglife.wordpress.com**

Journal

_____

_____

_____

_____

_____

_____

_____

_____

_____

_____

_____

_____

_____

_____

_____

_____

_____

_____

From my Heart and from the Creator
Right Now and in every moment
Every cell of my body
Every level of my consciousness
Every area of my Being
And every part of my mind
With expressed appreciation and Joy
I am living the blessings of the energy, essence
and quality of Life
That caused me to even more Love and adore my inner spirit
and my inner resources
For consistently having
My mind, influence, inspiration, support, assistance, guidance,
perceptions, decisions, choices, thoughts, actions, words,
feelings, behavior, and imagination
Based on the inner guidance and power of my Heart
The powerhouse of God's intelligence, love and energy
And Spirit acting on them so that I am always
Showered with some unforeseen good, blessings, benediction
Having more than I can possibly conceive
Having me radiate with goodness and Godliness
And through this Heart powered consciousness
I am the living proof of feeling with the sight of my Heart
Inspiration of a deeper sense of intuition
The emotional rewards of unconditional Love
Amazing brilliance, wisdom, and passion
Powerful and purposeful intention
Utilizing my unique gifts, strengths and talents
And having my spirituality with simplicity and elegance
Thank you Spirit.

—Comfirmation by **Al Diaz**

Review of The Titus Concept

The inspiration of the actual steps of The Titus Concept came to me in August 2005 and were stated in my original book "The Titus Concept Money For My Best and Highest Good". The premise of this book you are reading is still based on The Titus Concept and I have made it even more empowering with new insights that I will introduce at a later chapter.

For those who already kNow and understand the steps of The Titus Concept, the review this chapter provides will bring even more permanence of the steps within you. For those who are seeing these steps for the first time, it is very important that you understand what is BEing said within this chapter. The higher level of awareness that we all seek begins with these steps.

Let's begin…

What is your Life like?

Is your Life exactly how you thought it would be?

Would you like to have the freedom to create the

Lifestyle you desire and require?

If you are ecstatically happy with what your current external reality is, I congratulate you!

If you, on the other hand, would like to see, hear, and feel a difference in your external reality, then keep reading.

There is incredible value in The Titus Concept.

The value of increasing your awareness.

The value of BEing empowered.

The value of personal freedom in all areas and all levels of your Life.

The value of having the Lifestyle you desire and require.

The value of shifting your perception of your past.

The value of shifting your focus for the future.

The value of changing your internal well being for the present moment.

The value of a changing external reality that you desire.

That is incredible value.

So the next question is:

How much do you value your Self?

Do you value your Self enough to move forward?

Do you value your Self to have the Lifestyle you desire and require?

Do you value your Self that you know you deserve the best and highest good?

Exceptional value:

The Titus Concept will deal with fear directly.

The Titus Concept will lead you to heal, to forgive, to let go, to release, to shift, to change all that no longer serves you.

The Titus Concept will lead you to your true power of who and what you are.

Step #1 Shift the Perception (The past)

Where does judgment come from?

From a perception.

Where does perception come from?

From an experience that is accepted as valid or as truth.

Where is that or any experience stored, apparently forever?

Ego.

That sums up your past in a nutshell, and I will add that there is no way you can change your past. But what you can do is shift your past, or more accurately, the perception of it. To help you get through this step, remember that in every moment there is either an opportunity or a blessing.

Here is a scenario:

You are in a relationship in high school and for whatever reason you end up getting hurt in that relationship. A few years later, you're in your twenties and in another relationship. Again, it doesn't work out. Fast forward a few more years. Perhaps you are in a marriage, and it's not going so well. Do you see a pattern? For some of you, it may have happened several more times than this—like it did for me for the first forty years of my Life. Some of you may even blame or fault others or sometimes even yourself, just like I did. Blaming and faulting yourself and others is exactly the same as giving your power away. Unfortunately, some people never realize this.

Another scenario:

Your teacher in grade school who just adores you tells you "You are a success", but when you get to high school it takes a lot of effort to graduate, and college becomes a struggle to finish. Perhaps you ended up in career that was somewhat easy to get into, but not fulfilling. Through it all, in the back of your mind, you're wondering what is going on, even telling yourself "I know I should be successful!" Eventually you might even tell yourself "If it wasn't for this or that I might have (fill in the blank)." It's the blame game again, in a different form.

Yet another scenario:

When you're young you are told that arthritis runs in your family. Sure enough you go to a family gathering and you see some of the elderly folk slowly moving around, proving to you that what you were told is accurate. As you get older, you hear your parents complaining about their back pain. Maybe you get in a car accident and the doctor tells you "you will have arthritis by the time you are thirty five due to your injury". Well according to all of this information you are definitely going to have arthritis when you get older. So you start playing the blame game yet again: "If it wasn't for my family or the car accident…"

I am sure you have your own scenarios. But, with each experience you arrive at a perception, which you store in your ego, and then use it later in Life to judge the next experience or possibilities that may happen.

How in the world are you going to move forward when you are using these types of experiences to deal with what is going on in the present or planning for the future?

Here are some processes I have used with varied degrees of success. I'll use the above first scenario of emotional hurt from relationships.

Let it go or release it: I am letting go of this relationship, I am releasing the hurt. I am giving it all to the Universe. Six months later why am I still angry? Or did I just bury it deep inside of me and merely put it out of mind?

Heal: I am in sincere prayer or meditation mode to heal the hurt, but every time I do, I feel the hurt and pain all over again. I can't finish my prayer or meditation. I am determined to try again tomorrow.

Forgive: I sincerely tell myself that I forgive myself for messing up that relationship. But the dialogue continues: "That was a really dumb thing I did, but I forgive myself. I can't believe what I did! Why would I do something stupid like that?!! Stop! You're supposed to be forgiving your Self. Okay, settle down and start over."

Bury it and forget about it: Ten years later thinking I have moved on from the memory, something triggers it again in my current relationship, amplifying even more what I am going through. I start thinking, "Here I go again..."

All of those processes do work at varying degrees, and I have had prior success with all of them. However, but they do require a certain amount of effort. How about we move on to an even more effortless way that is also powerful?

Now say this:

Right Now, and in every moment, in every cell of my body, in every level of my consciousness, in every area of my BEing, and in every part of my mind, that "relationship" is for my best and highest good. Thank you Spirit.

What have you done?

You have shifted the energy of that relationship. You have told the Universe and your Self that regardless what transpired, it is for your best and highest good. Even if you only shifted the energy a small degree, you have made progress to be able to forgive, heal, let it go, or release it.

You can take it a step further and speed up the process of shifting the energy even more by telling your Self every time that specific relationship comes up, "This is effortless! This is simple! This is powerful!"

Some of you may be thinking, "How can I say that it was for my best and highest good when that other person almost literally destroyed my overall well being?"

Because it brought you to this moment… this moment of reading this book, this moment of an opportunity or a blessing, this moment to BE and this moment to move forward.

As you continue to say it is for your best and highest good, this is the vibration you will emanate, to which Spirit will respond. Remember The Law of Attraction. Your vibration will make it so, with the end result being for your best and highest good.

Do you understand?

Every instance, every circumstance, every experience, every situation and every moment of your past can be shifted to be for your best and highest good.

That doesn't mean you agree with what happened or even understand it (though you will understand later). Shifting all the junk as being for your best and highest good, completely stops the recycling process of the status quo. Your relationships will improve. Your success level will improve. Your health will improve. This shift will have a positive effect on just about every aspect in your life!.

Shift the energy!!! Remember everything is energy. Shift it Now!!! You can Now allow your Self to forgive, let go, release, and heal that which no longer serves you for your best and highest good.

Shift your perception (the past) as all being for your best and highest good, and you will stand on a foundation that will support you for what you desire and require.

Step #2 Shift the Focus (The Future)

Most of us use our past experiences to figure out what are we going to do in the future. We go back into our memory bank and find a similar experience of what we are trying to accomplish so that we can supposedly make an informed decision. The thing to note about that is we are basing our decision on our memory of the experience(s). So what happens when you are trying to accomplish something positive in your future, but the prior experience is supposedly negative?

On the other hand, there are some individuals that use their gut instinct or their intuition without giving any attention to their past experiences and just flat out succeed and accomplish what they set out to do...

Let's explore a simple and powerful way to be more like

the latter.

With step #1 you have shifted the perception—the past as BEing for your best and highest good. This means you have created a foundation to stand on, and you are Now functioning from that foundation. This emanates the energy of your best and highest good.

Let's go to the prior scenario of being told you were successful in grade school, but for whatever reason, the rest of your school years didn't work out that way. If you could, you would walk away from your current job.

If you did your homework and shifted your experiences of school, college, jobs that you've had, plus the current job you're in, as being for your best and highest good, you would be ready to focus on your future.

If someone was talking about you during your eulogy and you were able to listen, what would you want them to say about your success in Life? You wouldn't want it to be their definition of success, nor society's version of success, but your very own definition of success.

How would it feel?

What would you see?

How would you describe it?

What joy would it bring you?

What would you hear that person saying about your success in Life?

Now combine all those answers with those questions. That is your very own 'success story'. This is what you desire to BE. This is the end result, where you would tell your Self (if you could) that this is the value you brought into your Life. These are the specifics, the details of your 'success story', and Now you know what it looks and feels like.

Now say this:

Right Now and in every moment, in every cell of my body, in every level of my consciousness, in every area of my BEing, and every part of mind I am living and fulfilling my very own 'success story' for my best and highest good. Thank you Spirit.

Because you did step #1 and shifted all of your successful and unsuccessful experiences as being for your best and highest good, you were working from a foundation based on that premise. This makes it easier to accept and proclaim that everything relating to your success for the future as being for your best and highest good.

However your success story turns out, you must continue to proclaim it to be for your best and highest good. If you always remember to do this, then it shall BE. This becomes your vibration, and this is what Spirit will respond to. Spirit will match your exact vibration!

If for example, part of your success vision is to have a mansion, but ten years later you are living comfortably in a condo with no debt, what you have gotten is what you asked for. It is a 'success story' that is for your best and highest good. Nothing less and nothing more, but exactly for your best and highest good. Do you see?!! Spirit Loves you so much, it will give you what you are vibrating! Your only work is to shift your focus of your future to BE for your best and highest good in every area and every level of your Life including spiritual, mental, physical, and emotional well BEing.

Step #3 Change the Internal (The present)

Every one of these steps is important in its own way, but I believe this one is the most powerful, because it deals with the present moment. It is in this moment and in every moment that you create your Life. Remember the film that is running inside of you? From that film is what you create your Life from; the film that has all of your experiences, attitudes, beliefs, truths, feelings, emotions, thoughts and whatever else you have stored from your Life.

So guess what? Spirit loves you so much it will give you more of the same. Not because you don't deserve better, but because that is what you are sending out to the Universe in that moment. It is what the Universe will respond to.

So if you have shifted an area of your past as being for your best and highest good, and you have shifted the future of that same area of your life as being for your best and highest good, you can Now shift the present as being for your best and highest good.

It could be as simple as turning on a light switch, or telling yourself with every step you take that it is for your best and highest good. You can stub your toe (I know it hurts) and once you get over the initial pain, tell yourself that it is for your best and highest good. I have lost my footing and landed on my back going down the stairs of my home. As soon as I was able to catch my breath I started to say "This is for my best and highest good". Though it was painful at first, my back quickly recovered and the pain subsided, much to my amazement. When something like that would have happened before, it would have taken a few days for the soreness to go away. I am not stating this is a cure-all, I am simply telling you what it has done for me in my own Life.

Right now, in this moment, you have the opportunity to consciously and deliberately create the Lifestyle you desire and require. While you are going through your current experience, state that it is for your best and highest good, and it shall BE. You get to choose what each experience is going to BE. You do this simply by deliberately and consciously bringing into play all of your emotions, feelings, thoughts, actions, attitudes, and beliefs right into that specific moment, just by pausing and saying, "This is for my best and highest good". All it takes is a couple of seconds, and when it becomes automatic, you instantly just think it. That thought is still long enough to have you pause to create your Life in that moment.

What if things are currently happening in your Life that you wish would go away? Proclaim them as being for your best and highest good, and if it pops up again, then say it again. Trust me—whatever is happening will melt away.

It does so because you have raised your vibration and your energy level, by doing it in the most powerful moment that you DO have, which is right Now, and every ensuing moment.

There is nothing you can create with the moment that just passed. With the moment that has yet to come, you can plan for the future. But right Now you can dictate what you are currently going through; you can pick and choose what you desire this moment to BE. But here is the catch… you must be willing to take that pause.

Change the external (The creation)

This is the easiest step, because as you complete shifting by practicing the first three steps, your external reality automatically becomes shifted and changed. So this is really not a step, but rather a result of your work with the first three steps.

With everything you have done and read thus far, you have begun to take your power back. For some this may be a smooth transition, and for some it may be a bumpy ride, because your ego will not want to relinquish the power it has had all this time. Stand your ground, for you are the master of your Life. The time will come when your ego will be your servant and friend for your best and highest good.

Now having the foundation of the original three steps, it will be a smooth transition to move on to the next steps.

"BEing the Titus Concept is a simple, straightforward and profound manual for tapping into inner wisdom, guidance, and truth. It emphasizes techniques for shifting one's perception from the depths of victimhood and judgment to the transformational core values of self love, responsibility, empowerment, and living from the heart center. Titus instructs us to see all experiences as blessings or opportunities and provides a detailed and personal outline in which to do it. Readers of BEing the Titus Concept will learn how to transcend the past and create the future as they claim their power in the present moment. Don't miss this effortless guide to the alchemy of self-mastery."
—**Elizabeth Anne Hill, Author of "Twin Souls: A Message of Hope for the New Millennium" and co-creator of An Interview with the Universe www.interviewwiththeuniverse.com.**

Journal

Having the Lifestyle

Through this book and perhaps from other sources, you already know that everything in this Universe is energy, including us.

Everything I am about to tell you does work, and there are many who can tell you their success stories. But the main reason I am mentioning this is so that you can get a better understanding of what this book is about.

Creating and manifesting

You probably have been told that to have something in your Life you either have to create it or manifest it into your Life. Most of the following elements, if not all of them, are important to achieve success in creating and manifesting:

A vision

Goals

Emotions

Thoughts

Words

Actions

Visualization

Feelings

These all play a vital role in creating and manifesting what you desire and require in your Life. (Notice I didn't say want or need in your Life) That is why others say, 'be careful what you think about, what you say, and what you do', because the end result will be an exact match to what you think, say, and do.

Remember, everything is energy and like attracts like, so what you emanate is exactly what you will receive in return.

Does creating and manifesting work? Absolutely!

But for it to work, you must put forth a fair amount of energy and effort to create and manifest what you desire and require.

Let's go to an even more effortless way of receiving what you desire and require.

Attracting

You do this by getting clear on what you desire and require and magnetizing it to your Self. In other words, if you desire Peace in your Life, BE the Peace you desire and you will magnetize that Peace into your external reality.

So whatever is going on within you is what you are going to attract, because you are the magnet. That is the undeniable Law of Attraction.

I believe that attracting requires less effort than creating and manifesting, because instead of putting forth the energy and effort, you focus on the energy already naturally existing within your Self to attract what you desire and require.

Does the Law of Attraction work? Absolutely, every time, no exception!

It must work; it is a Universal Law.

The number one thing I had a problem with when I decided to create, manifest, or attract something into my Life was <u>doubt</u>!

Yes I did my positive thinking.

Yes I prayed.

Yes I had goals.

Yes I visualized, and even had a vision.

Yes I was careful with my thoughts, actions, emotions and feelings.

Yes all of that required a lot of effort!

Did they work? Yes, at varying degrees.

How about you?

What kind of end results have you had with creating, manifesting, or attracting?

"Al Diaz fills this guide to an awakened life with hope, encouragement and good will. He writes with the love and enthusiasm of a true seeker eager to share the treasures he has found."
—Mandy Evans, author of "Emotional Options" and "Travelling Free: How to Recover from the Past"

Journal

_____

_____

_____

_____

_____

_____

_____

_____

_____

_____

_____

_____

_____

_____

_____

_____

Having an Effortless Lifestyle

In the previous chapter, I have explained three ways for you to have the Lifestyle you desire and require: *creating, manifesting,* and *attracting.* You can achieve what you desire with all three of them, depending on how much effort and energy you put into them.

This brings me to the next approach that I believe is even more effortless than the prior three.

Allowing

When I finally understood this process, I thought I had it all. I felt like I hit the jackpot. It was something I was going to use to keep me permanently over the hump to have it all.

Each and every one of us is born perfect internally. In other words, we haven't lived to be influenced or corrupted by anyone or anything. If it remained that way, we would naturally live and function from our Heart's innermost desires, our own unique values, and our own inner Truth.

Simply put, we would allow what is already there. It would BE that simple.

But nobody really teaches us what we should or should not accept as truth in our Life, especially in our early years. As I have stated before. we go through our Life experiences and either consciously or unconsciously, we accept most of those experiences as "truth". That "truth" eventually becomes the "truth" which we end up living and functioning from. Yet, unless someone or something points it out to us, that is how we will continue to live—with these false "truths" that do not serve us at optimum levels for our best and highest good.

Remember, there is a way to deal with these experiences or false "truths" that ego holds onto so tightly. I explained this earlier in DOing the first step of The Titus Concept. The way to deal with this is by shifting the perception of the past—because most of us live and function from the foundation of our past.

Let's say that most of your Life you have had episodes of drama and Now you desire Peace. Acknowledge all of the instances of drama that you have had without blaming or faulting anyone or anything. As you go through each one, declare each episode as being for your best and highest good. You may be wondering, "Why would I do that?!" I'll tell you why. Because it brought you to this moment of right Now, and in every moment there is either a blessing or an opportunity. There are no other options.

As you go through each drama in your Life, acknowledging them and quickly shifting them as being for your best and highest good, you shift the energy of each episode and clear the path for the true inner Peace that resides within your Heart to emanate. It is the natural Peace that you were born with.

What happens then?

You effortlessly have more Peace in your Life, because you are allowing the Peace that *already* exists within you.

You see, in our Hearts we all have what we came here with—our values, our desires, our Truth. It is what Spirit provided us with, the seeds of who we are. It is what makes each of us unique and special. Even though what resides in our Hearts truly never goes away, it can be buried under all the junk we have accepted as Truth. This in turn feeds the ego, and the ego becomes where most people live and function from.

But the more you function from your Heart, the more you allow what you truly desire and require into your Life.

You *allow* what is already there.

So all of those months of shifting my past for my best and highest good, the Light of my Heart became more vibrant, and I emanated even more of my Heart's energy. My ego's role became reduced, and it started functioning more as a friend and servant. But understand that it was still a bumpy ride to get to that point with my ego, and even now at times I still deal with it.

As my Heart became more expansive and freer, I became more aware of my inner Self.

The seeds that were planted there long ago by the Creator of all creation began to sprout.

My unique and special gifts, strengths, and talents that I came here with, became even more prominent. I began to trust them even more. I began to exhibit the values I admired in others. Everything that was showing up in my Life was coming from my Heart because I was allowing what already existed within my Heart.

To me that was effortless…I thought I had hit the jackpot!

Try this:

Go to a mirror and look deep into your eyes (not at your eyes) and ask your Self "What three things would I like to allow my Self to have?"

Then write them down.

"Al Diaz has written a powerful and enobling book full of the warmth and graciousness of his loving heart! It helped me so much to clear limiting beliefs I wasn't even aware of at the time! Loving oneself unconditionally and embracing ALL the events in our lives allows us to easily flow into the life we only dreamed of before! All is well, so mote it be and so it is! All love,"
—Sandrabear of the Bear Clan (Multicultural Rainbow Shamanic Practitioner and facilitator of Sacred World Tours) www.sandrabearhealingarts.com

*"**BEing The Titus Concept,** by Al Diaz, is a very powerful resource and guide for personal growth and transformation - reminding us that the key to true success is loving and allowing what already is. With the tools and ideas in **BEing The Titus Concept,** you will quickly discover the truth and power that has been hidden inside you all along. Al Diaz has a masterful way of guiding us all to a place of great understanding and love for ourselves, our neighbors, and our Creator. This book is a must-read!"*
—Pete Koerner, author of The Belief Formula: The Secret To Unlocking The Power Of Prayer

Journal

Ultimate Effortless

In the previous chapters I talked about *creating, manifesting, attracting,* and *allowing.*

I believe as we went along from one method to the next, it became more effortless and less output of energy was necessary to have what you desired or required. Again, they all work, they are all successful methods. I know this because many individuals including my Self have used them all and have experienced varying success with each one.

I kNow that with what I am about to share transpired due to the fact I was allowing and functioning from my Heart and it became an opportunity to connect with both my own inner Wisdom and that of Spirit.

I had completed a powerful seminar in November 2006 both as a speaker and student, though I didn't really understand why then, my path began to shift soon after. I was allowing more and more into my Life, the relationship with my wife became beyond magnificent, and the gentle guidance I received caused me to focus on new paths. It was almost like it was time for me to take a break and BEing prepared to what I am about to share.

In mid December, Spirit decided it was time to introduce me to some more inspiration. Remember, I thought I had hit the jackpot by *allowing* the Lifestyle I desired and required.

Until this...

A major revelation that is so simple, it is absolutely mind boggling. How many times have we heard that to have something in your Life you must BE it? So using Peace as an example—to see and feel Peace in your Life, you must BE the Peace you desire and require.

I used to think, 'how can I be the Peace that I desire when there is chaos all around me? How can I be the Abundance that I desire when I only have a few hundred dollars to circulate?' I can go on and on.

It's like we are being asked to be something that is completely opposite of what we believe we are seeing in our external reality. Actually, this is exactly what we are being asked to do. So how do you feel Love in your Life when you are lonely? How do you express commitment when your habit is procrastinating? How do you wake up happy when you go to sleep sad?

So the burning question is: how do you consistently BE something that you do not yet have, or that you have not yet experienced?

Some will tell you to fake it until you make it. For instance, smile even though you are sad, or love others even though you are hurting inside. Does this work? Yes it does. I have smiled when I was sad and it would perk me up temporarily. I have loved when I was hurting inside and it would feel good to some degree temporarily. It takes a lot of effort to BE something that has yet to arrive in your reality. Does it work? Yes it does. But for me, it works in varying degrees.

Are you ready for ultimate effortlessness?

Are you ready to have the Lifestyle you desire and require?

I am going to use this book as an example, and one of my core values that I stated earlier, to go through this process.

Before I continue, you must understand these three very important things that I mentioned earlier:

1. The most powerful moment in your Life is right Now. Not the moment that is yet to come, or the moment that just passed, only the moment happening right Now.

2. BE thankful with Love and Gratitude for everything you have.

3. Finally, everything that exists in front of you has to come from within you first.

With this first example, I chose the value 'Harmony' and this book for this process.

Ready?

Say the following sentence:

I am allowing and BEing the Harmony this book represents for my best and highest good. Thank you Spirit. (or thy will be done)

Here are some examples of the Harmony in that declaration:

The Harmony it took for someone to envision and come

up with the idea of a book

The Harmony it took to get others to buy into the idea of a book

The Harmony it took to create the very first book from scratch

The Harmony it took for a book to BE read worldwide

The Harmony it took for Al Diaz to write this book

The Harmony it took for Al Diaz to have the resources to write this book

The Harmony it took for the change of hands to get this book in front of you

The Harmony it took for you personally to read this book

The Harmony of Divine Order for all this to happen

I am allowing and BEing the Harmony this book represents for my best and highest good. Thank you Spirit. (or thy will be done)

This book in front of me cannot exist in my reality unless it was already somewhere within me, and since everything is energy, the energy of Harmony that it took to get it in front of me is already an integral part of me. What does that mean? It means that I already have the Harmony within me because it could not exist if I didn't!!! Do you understand? Every bit of Harmony it took to get this book in front of me, I must already have within me right Now, in order for it to exist in my reality. Not one single degree of Harmony can be missing from within me because it must match the Harmony vibration it took to have it in front of me. It comes from within me first.

I am allowing and BEing the Harmony this book rep-
resents for my best and highest good. Thank you Spirit.
(or thy will be done)

With that statement, I am telling the Universe and my
Self who and what I am. I am affirming and confirming to
the Universe and to my Self, what my Truth is within me. I
am emanating that energy of absolute Truth to the Universe
with my declaration. I am DOing this in the most powerful
moment which is right Now.

I am allowing and BEing the Harmony this book rep-
resents for my best and highest good. Thank you Spirit.
(or thy will be done)

I am expressing my gratitude through my words. I am
expressing Love by recognizing the Harmony it took to get
this book front of me. (That doesn't mean I need to figure
out every bit of Harmony it took.) Finally, I am telling Spirit
in gratitude 'You are the Harmony.'

How about we try a value and something we have everyday?

Let's try the value of success and your home.

Ready?

Say the following sentence:

I am allowing and BEing the Success my home repre-
sents for my best and highest good. Thank you Spirit. (or
thy will be done)

Here are some examples of the success in that declaration:

The Success it took for the developer to bring all the finances together to build it

The Success it took for the manpower to build it

The Success it took for the local government to issue permits to build my current home

The Success that at one time it passed all inspections

The Success that I found my home and it found me

The Success that it is my home at least for Now

The Success that my family and I have a roof over our heads

The Success that it all happened in Divine Order

I am allowing and BEing the Success my home represents for my best and highest good. Thank you Spirit. (or thy will be done)

Again, my home cannot exist in my reality unless it was already somewhere within me, that includes the energy of my home, along with the energy of Success that it took to create my home before I even moved in. What does that mean? It means that I already have the Success within me because it could not exist in my reality if I didn't!!! Is it sinking in? Every iota of Success that it took to have this home had to match Success already within me in order for it to exist in my reality. Guess what? You can find Success or any value with everything in your reality, because it all comes from within you for it to BE there! You already have it!!!

I am allowing and BEing the Success my home represents for my best and highest good. Thank you Spirit. (or thy will be done)

With that simple statement I am telling the Universe and my Self who and what I am. I am affirming and confirming to the Universe and to my Self what my Truth is within me. I am emanating that energy of absolute Truth to the Universe through my declaration. I am DOing this in the most powerful moment which is right Now.

I am allowing and BEing the Success my home represents for my best and highest good. Thank you Spirit. (or thy will be done)

I am expressing my gratitude in words of understanding. I am expressing Love by recognizing the Success it took for my home to BE in my external reality. (That doesn't mean I need to figure out every bit of Success it took.) Finally, I am telling Spirit in gratitude 'You are the true Power of Success.'

Would you like to try another value with a person?

Let's use Caring and Mother Theresa.

Ready?

Say the following sentence:

I am allowing and BEing the Caring that Mother Theresa represents for my best and highest good. Thank you Spirit. (or thy will be done)

Here are some examples of Caring in that declaration:

The Caring between a couple to have a child name Theresa

The Caring of the Universe to have someone like Mother Theresa walk among us

The Caring she was guided with, enabling her to emanate that same vibration

The Caring of others who supported her through Love and prayers

The Caring of others who gave their resources and money to support her

The Caring she showed humanity for the best and highest good of all

The Caring of her own inner spirit

The Caring she showed as an example for all to see

I am allowing and BEing the Caring that Mother Theresa represents for my best and highest good. Thank you Spirit. (or thy will be done)

I must have the vibration and the value of Caring within me to understand its connection with Mother Theresa. Do you know why some don't see her in the same light? Their vibration doesn't match. I understand, see, and feel it; therefore my vibration matches the Caring that she emanated. It must BE within me for that to happen!

I am allowing and BEing the Caring that Mother Theresa represents for my best and highest good. Thank you Spirit. (or thy will be done)

Simply put, I am telling the Universe and my Self who and what I am. I am affirming and confirming to the Universe and to my Self what my absolute Truth is within me. I am emanating that energy of absolute Truth to the Universe through my declaration. I am DOing this in the most powerful moment which is right Now, and simply stating that I DO Care about my Self.

I am allowing and BEing the Caring that Mother Theresa represents for my best and highest good. Thank you Spirit. (or thy will be done)

I am expressing my gratitude in words of understanding, and that I DO see the connection. I am expressing Love by recognizing the Care that Mother Theresa represents for all creation. (That doesn't mean I need to figure out every bit of Care that it is) Finally, I am telling Spirit in gratitude, 'You have shown me how much you Care.'

Would you like to try another value with a daily ritual?

Let's use Abundance and a cup of water.

Ready?

Say the following sentence:

I am allowing and BEing the Abundance a cup of water represents for my best and highest good. Thank you Spirit. (or thy will be done)

Here are some examples of the Abundance in that declaration:

The Abundance it took for someone to create that specific cup in my hand

The Abundance the water represents coming from the original source or the creator of all creation since the beginning of time

The Abundance of turning on the faucet and instantly filling my cup with water

The Abundance of hydrating every cell of my body to keep me moving forward

The Abundance of others to bottle it and have it almost anywhere

The Abundance I have to buy water

The Abundance the water represents in giving Life as I drink it

The Abundance the water is, because that is what my physical being is mostly made up of

The Abundance of water that covers nearly 70% of the earth

I am allowing and BEing the Abundance a cup of water represents for my best and highest good. Thank you Spirit. (or thy will be done)

Water is abundant, it is everywhere. The earth is covered with water, from streams to oceans. Your body is mostly water. What does that tell you? That your vibration of Abundance has to match the Abundance of water that is in your reality! It could not exist in my reality unless it was already somewhere within me, so the energy of Abundance must BE there! What does that mean? Unless you can't actually see, taste, hear, touch, smell, or sense water, we are abundant! Water is everywhere! Every day I can see it, I can taste it, I can hear it, I can touch it, I can smell it, and I can sense it, because the abundance of water is the same abundance that is within me! Do you get it?!! Somewhere within me the vibration of Abundance has to be high enough to have all this water around me. Otherwise, if I had scarcity as a high vibration I would barely notice the water, if at all. Remember, you can find Abundance or any value with everything in your reality, because it all comes from within you for it to BE there! You already have it!!!

I am allowing and BEing the Abundance a cup of water represents for my best and highest good. Thank you Spirit. (or thy will be done)

I am telling the Truth to the Universe and my Self of who and what I am. I am affirming and confirming to the Universe and to my Self what my absolute Truth is within me. I am emanating that energy of absolute Truth to the Universe through my declaration. I am DOing this in the most powerful moment which is right Now.

I am allowing and BEing the Abundance a cup of water represents for my best and highest good, thank you Spirit. (or thy will be done)

I am expressing my gratitude in words of understanding, and that I DO see the connection. I am expressing Love by recognizing the Abundance that water represents for all creation. (That doesn't mean I need to figure out every bit of Abundance that it is) Finally, I am telling Spirit in gratitude, 'You are the true supplier of Abundance.' With these simple words: Thank you Spirit. (or thy will be done)

Now you try it. Pick a core value and any object or person, write it out and fill in the blanks. Then journal how you feel and what it does as you say it.

Go ahead!

I am allowing and BEing the _____ that_____ represents for my best and highest good. Thank you Spirit. (or thy will be done)

> Aloha Al,
> "You rocked my world with the simplicity, beauty, wisdom and love that I found contained in BEing the Titus Concept. As I continued to read and reread "for my highest and best good" I finally realized that it was a process of forgiveness, or in Hawaiian terms, ho`oponopono (making things truly correct) which is an ancient practice of our islands and one which kept us all living with Aloha or love.
> The other thing I noticed was that when I took the time to write and answer the questions posed in the book it answered the question most often heard from people spiritually awakening and that is "What is my purpose here on this planet?" and at the same time brought clarity and focus to the values and true desires of my heart. It would take a book larger than this one to convey my appreciation and love to you for BEing willing to allow yourself to share this wisdom with us all." Ke akua aloha pu me oe (The God of Love BE with you).
> **—Reverend Pomaika`i Coulon**
> **Kealakekua, Hawai`I www.weddings4love.com**

> "If you don't want to have your life transform, don't pick up this book! Simply reading Being the Titus Concept from cover to cover casually answering the questions was thought provoking and AHA inspiring. There are so many techniques and exercises, each one building upon the previous. That final affirmation sent waves of energy through my body similar to what occurs when I am in deep meditation."
> **—Llenar Bragg, Host, No Out There Talkshow**
> **www.no-out-there.com**

Journal

BEing The Titus Concept

With the last chapter I introduced to you the inspiration that came to me in December of 2006. I wasn't sure at first, but as I practiced it, I soon realized that it empowered and simplified The Titus Concept.

Within days of starting this new practice I was given an opportunity to spend the last days of 2006 and the first days of 2007 in Kauai, Hawaii with my wife. Ten days in paradise for about 75% below normal cost! I told my Self WOW, and I knew this was a gift from the Universe that was given to us.

On the flight over to Hawaii I started saying to my Self confirmations like:

I *am allowing and BEing the Power this plane represents for my best and highest good. Thank you Spirit.*

Or

I *am allowing and BEing the Wealth all of these people represent for my best and highest good. Thank you Spirit.*

By the time we landed in Hawaii I was on fire! From that point on I took as many moments as possible to notice what was around me. It was an opportunity to show my Self and the Universe that I understood what is really within me.

Within the first few days I was guided to refine what I was saying even more and have it more focused and direct. I began stating the confirmation of my inner kNowing without the fear. The following are only a few examples of what seemed to be hundreds of opportunities that I took to confirm to the Universe and to my Self the understanding of what is within me, and I repeated each one often.

I am allowing and BEing the Power of the ocean for my best and highest good. Thank you Spirit.

I am allowing and BEing the Life Force of the ocean for my best and highest good. Thank you Spirit.

I am allowing and BEing the Effortless nature of the waves in the ocean for my best and highest good. Thank you Spirit.

I am allowing and BEing the Growth of the vegetation around me for my best and highest good. Thank you Spirit.

I am allowing and BEing the Freedom of the birds that are flying by me for my best and highest good. Thank you Spirit.

I am allowing and BEing the Intimacy that my wife is showing me for my best and highest good. Thank you Spirit.

I am allowing and BEing the Love that people were giving and showing me for my best and highest good. Thank you Spirit.

I am allowing and BEing the Generosity that was given to my wife and I for my best and highest good. Thank you Spirit.

I am allowing and BEing the Creativity of the beautiful

sunsets for my best and highest good. Thank you Spirit.

I am allowing and BEing the Connectedness with the dolphins around me for my best and highest good. Thank you Spirit.

I am allowing and BEing the Success of a $2,000 hotel room per night for my best and highest good. Thank you Spirit.

I am allowing and BEing the Wealth of a beach front property home for my best and highest good. Thank you Spirit.

I am allowing and BEing the Harmony of Life and all is in perfect Divine Order for my best and highest good. Thank you Spirit.

I am allowing and BEing the accelerated Awareness of my new understanding for my best and highest good, thank you Spirit.

All of the above declarations had to BE somewhere within me in order for me to think them and speak them. Otherwise the thoughts would have never come; the words would have never been spoken. That means I already have all of the stated values!

With those declarations:

I am confirming to Spirit or the Universe who and what I am. Remember I asked how much do you Love your Self? I am telling Spirit how much I love my Self with those declarations! So Spirit, who Loves me so much, will give me *exactly* what I emanate in return!

I am deliberately and consciously telling and confirming to my Self who and what I am, so that every level of my consciousness, every area of my Being, every cell of my body, and every part of my mind is following the Truth I am expressing, as the master that I am.

I am co-creating with Spirit or the Universe because as I express them, I am using all of my senses, my emotions, my feelings and my inner spirit; and in DOing it in that moment while I am going through the experience, I am DOing it *precisely* when I have the most deliberate Power; *in that moment.*

This is **BEing The Titus Concept.**

By declaring the values that are important to you with everything and anything around you, is a confirmation that you realize that your vibration is a match with that value, and that it is for your best and highest good, because you stated it is.

You can look at a mean junk yard dog and say *'I am allowing and BEing the Blessing that dog is for my best and highest good. Thank you Spirit.'* What are you focusing on? What are you agreeing to? What are you accepting? What are you connecting to? The answer to all those questions is simply this: *Blessing.* Everything else becomes a distant third, including a 'mean junk yard dog'.

As soon as you finish saying thank you Spirit or thy will be done, in that moment your declaration, your confirmation, becomes for your best and highest good with the value stated from your Heart.

In that moment you are 'BEing The Titus Concept'

Now you try this empowered version. Pick a value and an object, situation or person and fill in the blanks. Write it out, and then journal what comes to you.

I am allowing and BEing the _____ that _____ is for my best and highest good, thank you Spirit.

Journal

BEing

Let's say that today you used the value Happiness five times in different instances, next week you are DOing it ten times a day, and by the end of 30 days you are DOing it a hundred times a day.

On the 30th day what do you think your focus would automatically BE on? What innate core value would you see everywhere? What energy would you emanate? What would you allow and BE? What energy would Spirit vibrate and give back to you?

HAPPINESS!

Can you imagine what you would BE if you did it several hundred times a day?

At that point, you would almost always BE consciously and deliberately living in the Now or in the moment, which you already kNow is where all the Power exists. You would function from your Heart's innermost desires and DO it with Purpose.

In that moment you are BEing the fullest and grandest

expression of who you are and what you are, you would BE fulfilling the status of what the Creator of all creation intended you to BE.

You would be using the seeds of your inner core values that you came here in this Life with, to have the Lifestyle you desire and require, and all BEing for your best and highest good.

I was doing a workshop in Arizona and one of the participants had pointed out to the group a very powerful insight. I have added to it as well.

All of these inner core values were put there by something or someone, and I am going to say the Creator of all creation. So that means they were put there out of Love, perhaps as a gift, or a tool, or maybe both.

Now picture a strong and durable piece of rope that can hold up to anything. Imagine that each strand of that rope is one of your core values. In other words, each strand that makes up the rope represents one of your core values. As you strengthen each strand by consistently emanating a different core value, the rope becomes stronger and more durable.

Do you know what is becoming stronger and durable?

Do you know what that rope represents?

Do you know what each strand of core values add up to?

LOVE

Let's pick three core values: Success, Joy, and Harmony.

When you see Success, Joy, and Harmony in all things and everywhere regardless of what is going on around you, you become Success, Joy, and Harmony. Therefore, that is what you emanate or vibrate. Well guess what? Spirit will give you back exactly what your vibration is, which in this instance would be Success, Joy, and Harmony. You would be co-creating your own blessings with the Universe and as long as you stayed in this mode, you would continue to BE blessed, and the cycle would continue.

What is this cycle called?

LOVE

Remember this: Spirit Loves you so much, it will give you exactly what is going on within you.

Strengthen your rope, by strengthening the strands of your core values. You can do this by BEing The Titus Concept and confirming to your Self and the Universe that your core values already exist within everything around you.

It is time and you deserve it.

Suggestion: Focus on your three most important core values for the first thirty days and journal your thoughts.

"In his book, BEing the Titus Concept, Al Diaz beautifully expresses THE essential truth: As you learn to love yourself unconditionally, the heart awakens. You connect to your divine essence. You're more successful at attracting what you "desire and require."
If you seek support in learning to live from the heart, as you create a peaceful, harmonious, joyful, abundant life, read the book. Lead yourself through the clear, powerful, activations and lessons. You'll love the results!"
—**Kathryn Jensen www.BlueDolphinEssences.com**

Journal

From my Heart and from the Creator
Right Now and in every moment
Every cell of my body
Every level of my consciousness
Every area of my Being
And every part of my mind
With expressed appreciation and Joy
I am living the blessings of the energy, essence
and quality of Life
Of even more loving and adoring my inner spirit and my
inner resources
For the support to have caused me as I speak this
The beginnings, manifestation and fulfillment of
Newfound levels of inner creativity
Utilizing newer energies within me
Perpetual act of Loving Self renewal
My external reality as new and healed at optimal
and joyous levels
Discovering newer dimensions that represent liberation
Arriving at newer, higher, raised levels of awareness
New, powerful and joyous healing and empowerment
My Life even more prepared and ready for the magnificence
that I already am
Living another of my Heart's inner most desires
Having another joyous reality that is even more
pleasant than any before
Thank you Spirit.

—Comfirmation by **Al Diaz**

Resources

There are many books I have read and people I have listened to, and I would say every one of them has guided me to remember even more who I am and what I am. Each one contributed with their guidance to help get me to the point where I am Now.

The following inspired me for this chapter:

Inspiration: Your Ultimate Calling by Dr. Wayne W. Dyer

Zero Limits: The Secret Hawaiian System for Wealth, Health, Peace, and More by Joe Vitale and Ihaleakala Hew Len, PhD

Busting Loose From the Money Game: Mind-Blowing Strategies for Changing the Rules of a Game You Can't Win by Robert Scheinfeld

I am not going to tell you what each book is about, though I do highly recommend that you read them. What I will tell you is that I found common threads with all three books as well as the one that you are Now reading.

As I had indicated in prior chapters, as you raise your level of awareness… guidance, resources, support, assistance, energy, insights, "ahas", and even more Love will come into your Life.

After rereading the original version of "BEing The Titus Concept" and the other three books listed above, I was struck with huge and major insights that caused my palms to sweat and my Heart to race.

Let me share an article I wrote for my monthly newsletter in August 2007, which will describe these insights in greater detail:

Blessings and Opportunities

by Al Diaz

Throughout most of my speaking engagements I have expressed that in every moment it is either a blessing or an opportunity and that any third option is not existent. Unless of course you wish to have a third, forth, or beyond that in options, because you do have free will and free choice.

But if your goal is to keep it simple and productive, and utilizing your Heart even more instead of your ego, then having every moment as a blessing or an opportunity is the way to go. But kNow that you co-create both of them and that every one comes from within you.

When a blessing comes into your Life it is something that you have brought into your Life either with ease or something you have "worked" towards. For example let's consider a blessing in the form of success in some part of your Life and it could be either small or big, as you consider it you may find that particular kind of success comes easy or natural to you. It just seems to happen naturally, almost like an inner kNowing that it is all going to happen the way it is supposed to. Another take of that blessing of success is an accumulation of understanding from all your prior experiences to finally getting it right to have a successful end result in that specific area.

You know what those prior experiences were?

Opportunities

With blessings you perhaps do what I do and that is to feel good, express gratitude, and look forward to your next blessing.

But with opportunities they are presented to you to remind you who you are, the wisdom that you have, and reclaim the power you have. An opportunity is an experience of possible growth as an end result.

Whatever your current situation is there are opportunities for you to have, it is all part of everyday living. For some they could be described as a challenge, a hurdle, an obstacle, a setback, or even a failure. Please note that I said they could be "described" that way, but that I still view them as opportunities, because that is what they are.

Everything in this Universe is here to grow, expand, progress, to move forward and express itself fully. It is the natural state of BEing. We as humans are the only ones that have free will and free choice to decide to move forward or not. That means we must consciously decide to move forward so that we may have deliberate outcomes. This means when an opportunity presents itself, we must utilize it to the best of our current ability. This is how we grow. As we put a string of opportunities to good use we create our blessings - the ones we have "worked" towards.

There are opportunities that may seem to be easier than others, or perhaps opportunities we feel we are not yet ready for. I have been there. In those instances I just proclaim them as BEing for my best and highest good. I do the best of my current ability to make the most out of them, and have faith that I am still moving forward.

Every utilized opportunity brings us further along our path of Self discovery and Self mastery. It is when we come to a realization of our power and our inner Wisdom that we eventually BEcome the fullest and grandest expression of who we are.

With the above article Now you kNow the detailed version of blessings and opportunities. From this book you Now understand that all of your external reality comes from within you and that the most powerful moment is right Now. You also Now kNow that everything is for your best and highest good.

Do you have an opportunity to utilize and grow or move forward with?

In the sentence below, fill in the blank with this opportunity. Then read the following sentences and pause between each sentence for a moment to let it sink in.

With this opportunity

_____:

I fully feel the energy of the experience

I am of Spirit, the power and essence of Spirit, and I have created this experience as an opportunity

I am sorry for this experience

Forgive me for this experience

I reclaim the power from this experience for my best and highest good Now

As I feel the surge, I feel my Self expanding into and expressing more and more of who and what I am, the status the Creator of all creation intended me to BE

I ackNowledge and appreciate my greatness to have this experience for my best and highest good

Thank you for the blessing

I Love you even more

To Now have every cell and DNA in my body, every level of my consciousness, every area of my BEing, and every part of my mind fully, newly, and optimally reborn for my best and highest good, to have resurrected my original innocence and power again. Thank you Spirit.

The pulsing of even more love in my heart right now is a huge success…

What did that do for you? How did it make you feel?

Journal your thoughts.

Journal

Now think of a blessing—it could be anything. When you do, fill in the blank of the following sentence, then read each sentence and pause between each one for a moment to let it sink in.

With this blessing

_____:

I fully feel the energy of the experience

I am of Spirit, the power and essence of Spirit, and I have created this experience as a blessing

I enhance my power for my best and highest good from this experience

As I feel the surge, I feel my Self expanding into and expressing more and more of who and what I am the status the Creator of all creation intended me to BE

I ackNowledge and appreciate my greatness to have this experience for my best and highest good

I am grateful for this blessing

I Love you even more

For having every cell and DNA in my body, every level of my consciousness, every area of my BEing, and every part of my mind fully, newly, and optimally reborn for my best and highest good, to freely BE my original innocence and power, thank you Spirit.

The pulsing of even more love in my heart right now is a huge success...

What did that do for you? How did it make you feel?

Journal your thoughts.

Journal

These are prayer like affirmations to your Self and to the Universe. They cause you to BE even more present in each moment. Every time you think of, see, or feel a blessing or an opportunity, you Now have a process to shift it for your best and highest good.

Whatever thoughts, insights, or "ahas" you journaled above, they are all perfect for you. Here is my explanation of each sentence and what they mean to me, but also know that you can reword them if you desire. The intention is to have you move forward and to live and function from your Heart.

For opportunities:

With this opportunity

_____:

I fully feel the energy of the experience

(Whatever feeling you have, good, bad, or indifferent, feel it to it's fullest extent)

I am of Spirit, the power and essence of Spirit, and I have created this experience as an opportunity

(You are expressing who and what you are, and that you have the ability to have created the experience)

I am sorry for this experience

(You are apologizing to your Self first, then all others for the experience)

Forgive me for this experience

(You are forgiving your Self, and asking for forgiveness from all others)

I reclaim the power from this experience for my best and highest good Now

(You are stating to your Self and to the Universe you are holding on to the power that created this experience. The important distinction is that you're not holding on to the experience but rather the ability to create it)

As I feel the surge, I feel my Self expanding into and expressing more and more of who and what I am the status that the Creator of all creation intended me to BE

(You are stating that you are BEcoming what the Creator of all creation desired you to BE)

I ackNowledge and appreciate my greatness to have this experience for my best and highest good

(Without blame or fault you are stating that you created this experience and with gratitude, you are recreating it as BEing for your best and highest good)

Thank you for the blessing

(You are showing your gratitude for this opportunity)

I Love you even more

(No matter what you still Love Your Self and others even more so)

To Now have every cell and DNA in my body, every level of my consciousness, every area of my BEing, and every part of my mind fully, newly, and optimally reborn for my best and highest good, to have resurrected my original innocence and power again, thank you Spirit.

(You Now have shifted the experience to bring your Self back to a clean slate)

The pulsing of even more love in my heart right now is a

huge success…

(With this process you Now have allowed even more Love to flow)

For blessings:

With this blessing

_____:

I fully feel the energy of the experience

(Feel the joy, the excitement, the peace, whatever it is to it's fullest extent)

I am of Spirit, the power and essence of Spirit, and I have created this experience as a blessing

(You are expressing who and what you are, and that you have the ability to create the experience)

I enhance my power for my best and highest good from this experience

(This blessing is the type of experiences you desire. Since you created it, you are stating that you have the ability to create even more)

As I feel the surge, I feel my Self expanding into and expressing more and more of who and what I am the status that the Creator of all creation intended me to BE

(You are stating that you are BEcoming what the Creator of all creation desired you to BE)

I ackNowledge and appreciate my greatness to have this experience for my best and highest good

(You are confirming to your Self and to the Universe of

the ability to create this blessing)

I am grateful for this blessing

(Gratitude!)

I Love you even more

(Keeping the Love flowing even more in all directions)

For having every cell and DNA in my body, every level of my consciousness, every area of my BEing, and every part of my mind fully, newly, and optimally reborn for my best and highest good, to freely BE my original innocence and power, thank you Spirit.

(To have experienced this blessing, it had to happen with a clean slate, and you're confirming it to your Self and the Universe.)

The pulsing of even more love in my heart right now is a huge success...

(With this blessing, Now the Love is really pumping!)

Do the explanations help? Do you see the differences between the two?

I know these are a little long to keep repeating throughout the day, but as you get comfortable with them and start seeing and feeling shifts in your Life, you can shorten or reword them, because eventually you will feel the process within you. It will become automatic.

With this chapter you Now have a Resource, and on the following page is a version you can have to carry around with you. So anytime you have an opportunity or a blessing to empower (which will empower you) just pull it out and DO it.

It is time and we deserve it.

For our best and highest good, all ways... In every moment.

With this opportunity

_____:

I fully feel the energy of the experience

I am of Spirit, the power and essence of Spirit, and I have created this experience as an opportunity

I am sorry for this experience

Forgive me for this experience

I reclaim the power from this experience for my best and highest good Now

As I feel the surge, I feel my Self expanding into and expressing more and more of who and what I am the status that the Creator of all creation intended me to BE

I ackNowledge and appreciate my greatness to have this experience for my best and highest good

Thank you for the blessing

I Love you even more

To Now have every cell and DNA in my body, every level of my consciousness, every area of my BEing, and every part of my mind fully, newly, and optimally reborn for my best and highest good, to have resurrected my original innocence and power again, thank you Spirit.

The pulsing of even more love in my heart right now is a huge success...

With this blessing

_____:

I fully feel the energy of the experience

I am of Spirit, the power and essence of Spirit, and I have created this experience as a blessing

I enhance my power for my best and highest good from this experience

As I feel the surge, I feel my Self expanding into and expressing more and more of who and what I am the status that the Creator of all creation intended me to BE

I ackNowledge and appreciate my greatness to have this experience for my best and highest good

I am grateful for this blessing

I Love you even more

For having every cell and DNA in my body, every level of my consciousness, every area of my BEing, and every part of my mind fully, newly, and optimally reborn for my best and highest good, to freely BE my original innocence and power, thank you Spirit.

The pulsing of even more love in my heart right now is a huge success…

"This delightful and succinct book nudges you to remember the wisdom you already possess. The included exercises provide fuel for contemplation, and encourage deeper exploration of your inner self."
—Mary Lee LaBay, Ph.D., author of Exploring Past Lives: Your Soul's Quest for Consciousness. www.maryleelabay.com

"Observing our lives through new eyes can teach us how life really works so we can attract our heart's desires. We humans are so creative! We've come up with dozens of complicated ways to delay or stop us from getting what we really want. Al Diaz's second book, BE-ing The Titus Concept, provides an easy-to-follow process designed to remind us who we really are in order to design and then live our best and highest lives. If you're willing to drop your story about why your life is the way it currently is in order to manifest the life you dream of living, then BE-ing The Titus Concept might be just what you've been waiting for."
—Sheryl Hirsch-Kramer Author, Nine Roses for Chelsea: a spiritual journey, Host, Glow With The Flow: Your Guide To Thrive, Survive, and Become More Fully Alive Radio Show www.GlowWithTheFlow.com

"I finished reading 'BEing the Titus Concept' with a big smile. With clarity, the message in this book inspires as well as motivates the reader constantly through every chapter. The techniques mentioned in the book are practical, achievable and progressive. It is delightful to see how much is given and how much may be received in so few words and the little time it took to read this book. Subtlety and Simplicity often go hand in hand in a powerful partnership. This partnership is naked, pure and omnipresent. Al's writing is both sincere and inspiring. The message in BEing The Titus Concept is Simple and Subtle."
—One Love
Santhan, Khanyi Media

Final Thoughts

Everything I have written on these pages comes from my Heart and the inner kNowing that I have been blessed with. It is the same type of inner kNowing that you have, only different in the sense of what you specifically have been blessed with. But kNow that Wisdom was placed within you for you to share, it is your gift to this world, it is how you add value, and it is what makes you so special.

With this book I am sharing my insights that come from my own Wisdom, that was finally awakened within me through the guidance of others.

Yes, to some extent we all must go through our own opportunities or "lessons". They are our unique path of Self discovery and Self mastery. It is through these unique experiences that we grow if we choose to do so, or limit our growth and Joy, remaining wherever we are at in our current lives.

But why would you want to do that?!! Because of fear? Because of low Self worth? Because you are tired or at the end of your rope?

I kNow for a fact that if you practice the "unconditional Love" mirror technique exactly as it is explained for thirty days, you will move forward from whatever is holding you back.

You will notice that you will begin DOing more positive things for your Self, that your Life will begin to shift and you will see a definite change in your external reality. Most importantly, how you see and feel about your Self will be remarkably different.

This book has given you many different ways to move forward, which is our natural state of BEing. Somewhere within your Heart is the desire to grow, to BEcome the status that the Creator of all creation intended for you to BE.

My intention with this book is to enhance what you already kNow, to guide you to remember what you already kNow, so that which no longer serves you for your best and highest good will melt away.

Very simply put, I am here to help guide you, perhaps to accelerate your awareness, and maybe empower you so you can feel the Love and Freedom of your Heart instead of fear. The best case scenario would be a combination of all three, because then you would have that inner kNowing and Trust that is desired and required for your own special journey in this Life to enjoy and complete.

As your awareness accelerates, as you feel empowered, as your freedom grows, and the Light of your Heart expands, remember the following affirmation and say it when you are ready…

I am allowing and BEing ALL THAT IS for my best and highest good

With this affirmation you are declaring that you are One

with Spirit.

One day I would Love to hear your story, or hear about your blessings or opportunities, because then you would be sharing with the world and guiding us to grow and move forward with your own special gifts, strengths, and talents. You would BE the spark for all others to see, the spark that would ignite what is within their Heart, and I kNow this to BE true just for you. Just listen to your Heart and it will BE.

With inner kNowing and complete Trust in Spirit, and until next time, I leave you with this:

I am allowing and BEing the Love that this book is for my best and highest good and for the best and highest good of all. Thank you Spirit, thy will BE done.

There is Now only one reason to seek, and that is to BE guided, because it is already within you…

Please go to my website and share your thoughts with me. I would Love to hear from you. Thank you.

Ilumine Ao,
Al Diaz
www.thetitusconcept.com

BEing The Titus Concept is a deeply profound and perfectly thought filled journey of one man's heart to the paths of wonder and completion. This book is the perfect gift to allow yourself to follow his heart into the inner depths of your own.
—Emalani, Visionary Instructor and Author

Spirit
I already am in total alignment
Utilizing the power of the Infinite
As a unique expression of the Infinite
With everything that I have
Conceived, expressed, stated, articulated, communicated,
and conveyed on these pages
All are acts of Love
And motivated by Love
Come from my Heart
Express Life
And are my deepest Truth
I have taken inspired action
Utilized my wisest thoughts
Efficaciously used my consciousness
Have everything going for me
And done what I have done
And all that I can BE
Which is more than enough and with grace
I surrender everything said on these pages to you Spirit
And I am serenely confident
And trust in the benevolence of the Universe
And kNow that whatever happens is totally worth it
And see the miraculous activity of God at work
Because it is what I desire and require for this process to
BE at every level
And simultaneously BE pulled towards and moving towards
The accomplished end results that are for our best
and highest good
Thank you Spirit.

—Comfirmation by **Al Diaz**